The Donkey Stone
&
Dolly Blue Days

Poems, Reflections by David Prestbury

Special edition
published by David Prestbury 2008
IBSN 978-0-9559777-1-8

Second edition published 2008 by Lulu.com
IBSN 978-1-4092-1881-4

First edition published 1998 by Castle of Dreams
Publishing Co. IBSN 1 86185 158 8

All Poems & Art work - Drawings & Illustrations
including Front & Back Cover designs are by the Author

All family photographs (apart from school archive Photo's)
are taken by the Author & the Author's
late father Alfred Prestbury
The Photo of David Prestbury 2008 on pg.87
Was taken by my Bro. Philip

For

My mum Winifred & late father Alfred
(For my upbringing & inspiration)

Daughter Laura Joanne

Sons: Damian Scott, Nicholas Alexander (& partner Lisa) & Jaimie Lee

Grandaughter: Robyn Alex & Grandson: Charlie Alan

My Brothers: Philip, Glyn, Duncan & Bryan & their families

Old street pals & School mates - this one's for you

MUM & DAD

These Poems, are reflections of my boyhood years
Set in the late fifties - on the streets
Where I lived & grew up

These for me were 'magic moments'
Which I'll treasure for the rest of my life
And savour with great affection

Day's that were simple, sometimes hard
But mostly very happy days

I hope you get as much pleasure as I did
Writing these nostalgic & memorable moments

'There's nothing like a bit of nostalgia
To stimulate the soul'

Or as someone once said –
"Nostalgia's not like it used to be".

Acknowledgement

Special thanks to my late father Alfred for the Photographic childhood memories - God bless!

Contents

BRO'S GLYN, MYSELF, PHILIP, DUNCAN & BABY BRYAN OUTSIDE OUR HOUSE IN BARRINGTON STREET, CLAYTON, MANCHESTER 1962

CLAYTON INDUSTRIAL ESTATE (1956 -1958)

The street where I used to live was of
'Coronation street' class
I remember those back to back -
Two up & two down terraced houses
And the scruffy kids that passed

Even today,
I can still smell and taste those odorous fumes and gases
From the local knacker yards, plants and foundries
And see those smoggy, smoky factories
That discoloured our houses and lungs

In the distance not too far away a certain time of day
You would hear the rhythmic booming of steam hammers
From the English steelworks pounding and pounding away

In the cold, wet, wintry months
That damp Manchester climate would cast
An atmospheric depression over the city
Depicting the austere drabness of our locality

Contrasting with the dark red brick terraced houses
With slime green or mucky brown front and back doors
Were grey slates, grey pavements, grey skies, grey pigeons
In fact everybody seemed ashen and grey

I, reflect on the brighter days
Especially those scorching hot, sweltering summer days
Around the parks and fields everywhere
The mixed aroma of freshly cut grass
(with a slight tinge of dog excrement) seemed to linger in the air

Day's of playing fields & pleasure grounds –
Belle Vue Zoo amusement park and fairgrounds

And on the freshly chalked pavements
Where the boys played buses and cars
And where the girls played hopscotch
With empty Kiwi shoe polish tins and jars.

Hopping , skipping – "
Salt!" "mustard!" – "vinegar! " - pepper!'"
"One potato!" - "two potato!" – "three potato!" – "four!"

As the little girls sat on the edgings watching in awe
Wearing mum's lipstick, old shoes and granny's shawl

Up in the air they throw and juggle with their 'two balls'
Showing off their 'bottle green' knickers when doing
Handstands against the end terraced walls

RAGBONE MAN

Down the back entries you'd hear the rickety rattle
Of the Rag & bone man's cart as he bellows "rrrraggggbone!"

Our mother would tear the shirt off my back
For the magic charm of a donkey stone!

- You see, she used to take pride
In our little front steps - our mother did!

Up and down with their handcarts they push and roll –
As Bob the 'lettuce man' - screams and bawls –

"Getcha fresh lettuces!" – "fresh celleree!" – "Eeenglissh tomatoes!"
His booming voice echoing off the back entry walls

BOB THE LETTUCE MAN

I remember the gypsies calling to our house
"Shhh! be quiet!' whispered our mother – "as a mouse!"
But sometimes around the back they'd sneak and creep

To catch us, tell our fortunes, sell us 'garden-picked flowers'
Pegs and little brown packets of lavender seeds
For a 'tanner' each - & we always bought at least two

Just in case they put a curse on the family
And mother being superstitious - Well you never knew - did you?
Then came those turbaned salesmen with sullen faces
Making their way up our streets carrying large tanned suitcases

Knocking on all our doors –
Unsuccessfully selling ladies nylons
And all kinds of brushes and brooms
For our backyards and linoleum floors
For them we never opened our doors

DAY'S OF THE OLD BACKYARD

In our backyards, as kids we'd often play
And swing on the washing lines - until one day
 Ours snapped & I fell & cracked mi 'ed
- "Swing on that bloody washing line agen!"
 Shouted our angry mother
 "& you'll go upstairs to bed!'

In our backyards, kids would create
Out of the odd orange box, trolley or mineral crate
Guiders, bogies, go-carts & sledges
& help our dads to mend, fix and paint
The little front garden gates & fences
Sometimes with any leftover bits of wood
We'd chop, bundle & sell firewood

Tops of coal sheds were littered & strewn with broken chairs,
old burst mattress's, rusty bike frames & other threadbares

Inside the out-houses & sheds (apart from the pigeon-cote)
You always found –
Living with the cat pee, coal & coke -
Guinea pigs, mice & hamster cages, rabbit hutches
Frog spawn, newts in jam jars -
Plus the odd frog or toad hopping around

& on that little outside Loo
Where we'd sit 'til our cold little bums turned blue
With only a paraffin lamp to keep us alive
Dithering & shivering trying to survive

Aye! there were no room for the squeamish & mard
Times were tough & times were hard
But we had many a good time in our old backyard

STREET GAMES

Have you any comics to swap?" – my best friend would call and say
"Thre'penny' war comics - Tobruk - El Alamein - Dunkirk and D-day
Those D.C's - Superman - The American league of justice – Batman
Casper the ghost - Sad Sack & Spiderman

And those 'one & three' classics - Man in the Iron Mask - Call of the Wild
The Red Badge of Courage - Treasure Island - Beauty and the Beast –
The Black Tulip - Coral Island - Silas Marner - Moby Dick
 20,000 Leagues Under the Sea - A Tale of Two Cities
 - But nobody wanted Zane Grey!

Then the ritual of comic swapping would prevail
Got! - not got! - got! - got! - not got! - not got! - was followed by
"'Are you coming out to play?" - 'I'll just ask mi ma!
"All right!' came the reply – "as long as you don't go far"
 So it's off down the street we'd go –
For a game of hide & seek or rallivo

"Sciss - pap- brick!' (scissors - paper - stone)
& I'm on again counting 10 - 20 - 40 - 60 - 80 -100 in vain
Shouting 'Coming out! - ready or not!"
Hunting, seeking, searching - until I find them

About half a mile away - on top of the garages they lay –
"Whip! Tommy! Whip! Joey" - all in! - all in! - den's off! one! two!-three!"
Half past nine & getting dark - bedtime nearing for Joey & me
Tommy say's 'lets go to the park' –
Tommy's older than us you see

"Awe! come on! let's run & hide whispers
Tommy naughtily
As we hear our mothers shouting -
"Better go!" - say's Joey to me,
"Or we may get a good clouting!'
And we'd run all the way home
To the sound of dad's loud whistle

BRO. DUNC, MYSELF, BABY BRYAN, BRO'S. PHIL & GLYN IN PHILIPS PARK,
CLAYTON,MANCHESTER,1962

THAT LITTLE CORNER SHOP

Up our street, just near the top
Where you would find us kids
Hovering like bees around a honey pot
All waiting anxiously excitingly
For that 'candy-striped' shutter' to roll up

And then,
As the doorbell rings & up it goes
We'd all pile in - in droves,
Pushing & pulling
Tugging & shoving each other
& with our 'tanner' spends - we would buy -

H'penny Spanishes & Kayli
Black Sambo's, Penny Chicks, Liquorice Sticks
Barley Sugar Sticks, Coltsfoot Rock
Spangles & Swaggering Dicks
Everton Mints, Trebor Mints,
Zubes & Tic-Tacs

Humbugs, Cough Candy , Victory 'V' Lozenges & Hacks
Rainbow Crystal, Sherbet Fountains & Dab's
American Cream Soda, Thre'penny Jamboree Luckybags

Parma-Violets, Flying Saucers, Frozen Jubblies
Toffee Cigarettes, Love Hearts, Penny Bubblies
Chewing Gum with transfers & football cards
Spangles, Tu'penny Nuggets & Penny Arrow Bars

Cinder Toffee, Palm Toffee, Coconut -Ice
Pea-nut Brittle, Bazooka Joe's, Chocolate Mice
Fry's Five Boys, Nuttalls Mintoes, Aniseed Balls
Blackjacks, Fruit Salads & Uncle Joe's Mint Balls
All for 'four-a-penny' -
Spending all our pocket money - until we haven't any

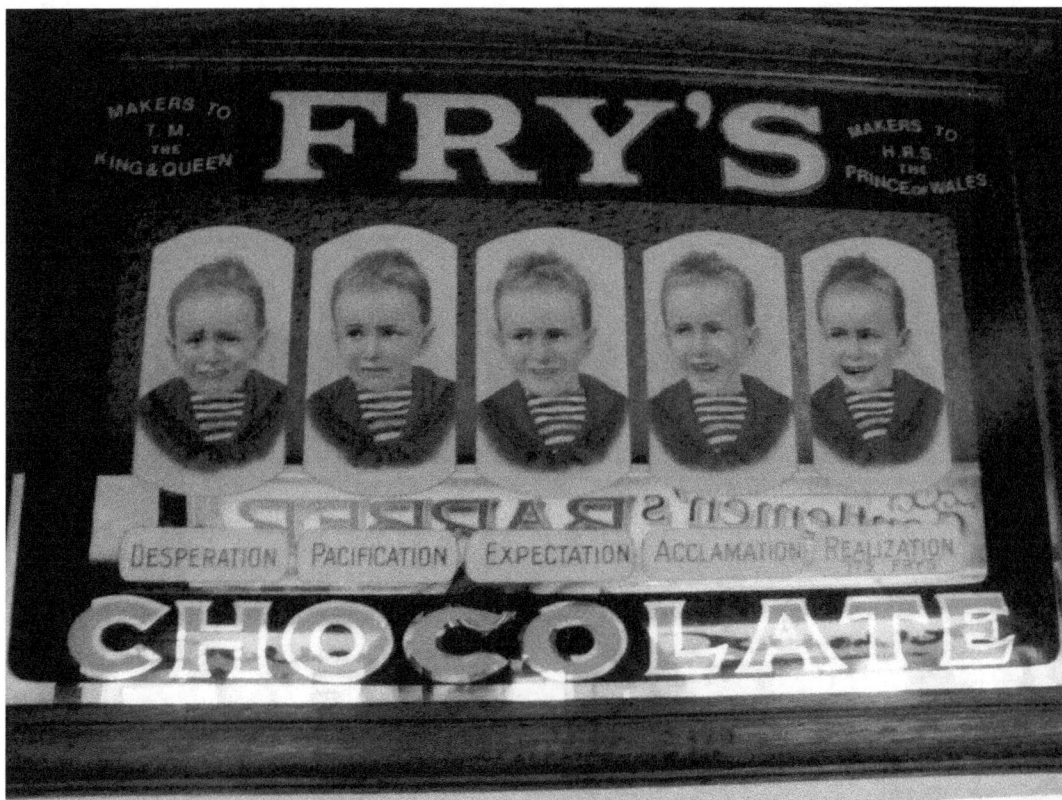

MY ATTIRE WOULD BE:

A green striped t-shirt
Khaki shorts with pitch on the arse-end
Held up with a 'snake-belt'
Grey socks with two red rings around the tops
A pair of baseball boots, gollies, (galoshers)
Plastic sandals or grandad's old shoes
And of course in wet weather or snow -
Welly's (Wellingtons) with the tops rolled down
- To save them smackin' the backs of your legs - red raw!'

OTHER STREET GAMES

Statues - Kick-Can - Whip & Top - Kingy
I draw a snake upon your back'
'What time is it Mr. Wolf ?' - Spin the Bottle,
True, Dare, Kiss, Command or Promise - I sigh!
Split the Kipper - Ticky it & Ticky off the ground
Flying Kites up in the Sky -
"Flee – Fly – Flo – Bang! - same as the Dummy's on!" was the cry

Cops & Robbers - War games on the croft
"Whose playin' cowboys and indian's? - all join on!"
Sang the kids with arms around each other's shoulders
Marching & beckoning for more contenders to join on -

"Alla balla booooosha! - who'se got the ball?" -
"I haven't got it! - I haven't got it! - who's got the ball?"
Playing Knights of the round table -
And who wanted to be Sir Lancelot - every tot!

MY LITTLE BRO. DUNC

Ivanhoe & William Tell –
"Come away, come away with William Tell
Come away to the land he loves so well" -
Remember 'Hamburger Gessler' -
Every fat kid was named after him

Robin Hood with Maid Marion
Little John & Friar Tuck -
Had us kids jumping out of trees
Fighting & rolling about In slutch & muck

"We are the Mystery Riders
That kill the Spiders
Upon the wa-a-a-all!" -
We'd sing & chant galloping down
The back entries

I remember one entry we used to call
The 'Death entry' - cos' it had a
Skull & Crossbones painted on the wall
In white ghoulish paint - 'whoooooooo!'
Which was quite scary at night.

STREET LIFE

Days of notorious criminals and villains
Like 'bare arse the bandit' from 'arse 'ole creek'
& 'Jimmy Greenteeth' whoever he was?
We were shit scared of him

The dares that made you shiver
Like balancing the 'one man bridge'
jumping and swinging (on a rope tied to the end of the tunnel)
across the 'Red River' (Medlock)

Or riding your bike without Brakes
Down 'Bunkers hill' in Daisy Nook (Failsworth)
To prove you weren't 'chicken' or 'yeller' -
Where you'd turn a deathly colour of white
Instead as you almost crashed
& fell headlong into the river
What a dare! what a scare! what a shiver!

I remember going to the local butchers
(Alwyn Griffiths - North road, in Clayton)
On Saturday mornings for a bucket of sawdust
- To mark out the 'red rec' football pitch
For our school matches

"If you tread on a crack - you'll marry a gnat,
And a beetle will come to your wedding"
Sang the young girls as they hopped & skipped
Inbetween the flagstones

As for my artistic talents
I would sit in the middle of the road
Popping pitch bubbles & making the most incredible patterns
In the black sticky pitch with my lollipop stick

And yet today - on our pavements
A thick blanket of Tarmacadam conceals our chalk-dust memories

MUM WITH BRO'S DUNCAN (LEFT) & GLYN (RIGHT)

BABY
BRO.BRYAN

POLITICS

My introduction to Politics
Was throwing apple cores & grass sods
At Oswald Mosely's fascist 'Blackshirts'
Whenever they appeared on our streets

MOLLY DANCING

Knocking on neighbours doors
Dancing, prancing & singing
"Molly dancers kicking all around" -
Dressed up in funny clothes with painted faces
With the elected 'May Queen' draped in old net curtains
Dancing around the makeshift 'May pole'

Adorned with coloured paper ribbons & tinsel
Collecting money for our 'street parties' -
"If you havn't got a penny - an h'penny will do
If you havn't got a h'penny - God bless you! "

PATRICK HERMANN (THE IRISH GERMAN?)

Was a mad spotty bespectacled young 'Scientist'
Who bottled 'human gas' into test tubes
For some weird & potty experiment.

He converted his Dad's garden shed
For his Laboratory tests
Dissecting newts was another speciality of his
& for an encore -

He would, with a wicked grin, put a straw up a frog's bum
Then blow as hard as he could
Thus exploding the poor creature into kingdom come
He was an evil little bugger with his bunsen burner
Was our Patrick Hermann the sadistic, spotty
Bespectacled mad Irish German?

KING KONG

Was another local character
Who lived in the same street as our Patrick
If you kicked your ball accidentally
Over his Garden wall -

He would charge out of his front door
Growlin' an' snortin' like a rampant Gorilla
With his metal spike as usual
Like a man possessed - spike your ball! -
A real nice friendly neighbour
& oh! such a lovely fellow

DONKEY STONE AND DOLLY BLUE DAYS

1958 was a sad year for our City
It was the year of the Munich air disaster
In which eight of our football heroes from 'Manchester United' perished
Roger Byrne, Mark Jones, David Pegg, Billy Whelan,
Geoff Bent, Tommy Taylor, big Duncan Edwards & Eddie Coleman
Memories of our great football team
Will forever & ever be cherished

I remember those donkey stone & dolly blue days
Days of parlours & glory 'oles
Grass sod raids - street games - crystal sets
Steam trains - Trolley buses - first T.V. sets
Barley stew - 'tater ash - pea soup (with ham shank!)
Stewed prunes - cod liver oil - bread and dripping
Tripe & onions - cowheel - jam & sugar butties - yuk!
Home-made rice pudding - I sigh!
'Save us the skin' was the cry

The Morton Fraser harmonica gang
The Nit-wits, the Crack-pots & the Crazy gang
Johnny Morris - the Hot Chestnut Man

We had slapstick comedy
Like Mr. Pastry doing his solo dances
The Boston two step and the Bengal lances
Norman 'Mr Grimsdale!' wisdom tearfully
Singing his signature song -
'Don't laugh at me 'cos I'm a fool'
'Cherry! You beast!' screeched Billy Bunter
The cad of Greyfriars public school

Charlie 'allo my darlings' Drake in –Mick & Montmorency
Jerry Lewis & Old Mother Riley had you in a frenzy
The hilarious - Benny Hill - Arthur Haynes - Ted Ray
Fat, monacled Fred Emney- Jimmy Edwards - Frankie Howard - Danny Kay
David Nixon & Tommy Cooper were magic
Terry Thomas, Peter Sellers, Tony Hancock (his suicide was tragic)

Johnny Morris who told 'Tales of the Riverbank'
And did animal impersonations
That pleased and tickled our Gran
Lenny the Lion with Terry hall

BABY BRO. BRYAN

Dixon of Dock Green - 'evening all!' –
Billy Bean & his funny machine
Macdonald Hobley - the original 'Mr. squeaky clean'
The Grove family - Britain's first soap
The Army Game with Bootsy & Snudge
Flogger Hoskins and Leonard Bone - what a dope!
The Larkins - 'Edddddy!' bellowed our Ada - alias Peggy Mount
The Rag trade with Miriam Karlin ordering 'everybody out!'

Sat up with a 'much larger than now!' Wagon Wheel
Toblerone or a Walnut Whip
A glass of Dandelion and Burdock or Ginger beer
Nervously watching - Quatermass & the pit
The Third Man with Harry Lime
The Four Just Men - conquerors of crime
Highway Patrol starring Broderick Crawford
No hiding place with Raymond Francis
Casebook – with Edgar Lustgartten
Maigret with Rupert Davies
Perry Mason with Raymond Burr
Sea Hunt with Lloyd Bridges

17

Armchair Theatre - The Phil Silver's show (Sgt. Bilko)
The adventures of Sir Lancelot - Roger Moore in Ivanhoe
Sunday night at the London Palladium
With "I'm in charge!!" 'Bruce Forsyth'
& the ever popular King Brothers singing -
"Standing on the corner - watching all the girls go by"
With a mischievous glint in their eye

The Beverly Sisters were the sweethearts of the day
Remember ventriloquist doll '- "Hello, I'm Daisy May"
Arthur Askey with his "Busy Busy Bee"
Armand & Michaela Denis those exciting explorers
Hans & Lottie Hass demons of the deep blue sea
Seventy Seven Sunset Strip - click! click!

And those corny game shows and quiz's like -
Beat the Clock - Spot the Tune - Criss Cross Quiz
64,000 Question - Double Your Money and Take Your Pick
Dr. Kildare with Jill Brown & Richard chamberlain
Emergency Ward 10 - Amos & Andy - Hullo deh! Saphiirre!

Dandy * Beano * Beezer * Topper * Lion * Tiger
Swift * Eagle * Wizzard * Hotspur

The Bash Street Kids - Desperate Dan - Dan Dare - hero spaceman
Keyhole Kate - Beryl the Peril - Minnie the Minx –
Big Fat Boko - Hungry Horace - Jonah the Jinx

Roger the Dodger
Winker Watson -
up to their pranks

General Jumbo with
His radio controlled
Army & tanks

Roy of the Rovers -
Did they ever lose?
The Knumbskulls -
Lord Snooty & his pals
Ginger
Little Plum (your redskin chum)

Black Bob - Korky the Cat - Mickey the Monkey
Pansy Potter - Biffo the Bear - Pop, Dick and Harry
The Hillys & the Billys shooting it out
Dennis the Menace - what a lout!

Max Wall & ol' rubber-neck Nat Jackley with their funny walks
Norman Evans 'over a backyard wall' were kings of the music hall
Those drunks - Jimmy Jewel & Freddy Frinton were intoxicating
Snozzle Durante 'dat ain't no banana! - dat's my dose!' was fascinating
Sitcoms like 'I Love Lucy' & 'I Married Joan'- were about as exciting
As 'The Potter's Wheel' or as stimulating as 'Brains Trust' with Gilbert Harding.

Watch with Mother with Andy Pandy & Looby Loo (& teddy too!)
Bill & Ben the Flowerpot Men - Muffin the Mule - Rag, Tag & Bobtail
The Wooden Tops (with the biggest spotty dog you ever did see!)
Michael Bentine's - Bumblies - One - Two & Three & Rolf Harris's – Willabee!

19

GREAT BALLS OF FIRE

When god created women -
From the sensuous & seductive
Miss Brigitte Bardot
Luscious Jane Mansfield,
Chesty Sabrina & Diana Dors
To the best Screen Goddess of all
The one & only Marilyn Monroe

& for the girls the handsome
Tony Curtis & Rock Hudson,
The rugged Kirk Douglas,
Burt Lancaster,& Charlton Heston
& those mean and moody heroes -
James Dean & Marlon Brando

Rebel without a cause - The wild one - The blackboard jungle
High school confidential - The girl can't help it
'Live fast, Die young' - being the teenagers statement

Days of chimney sweeps & hula hoops
Rock n' roll & skiffle groups
Brylcreamed quiffs - d.a.'s - sideburns - beehive hair do's
Beetle crushers, stiletto heels & blue suede shoes

"*Just walking in the rain*" cried Johnny Ray in emotional pain
 "*I'm a pink toothbrush - you're a blue toothbrush*"
Sang 'ol' big 'ed' Max Bygraves dishing out his usual trash!
As Guy Mitchell sat "*singing the blues*" &
'*She wears red feathers & a hoola hoola skirt -*
She lives on just coconuts & fish from the sea'

The stargazers sang "*I see the moon the moon sees me*"
As our parents nodded their heads side to side
'*Rock with the caveman*' raved Tommy Steele
As Frankie Laine roared "*Rawwwhide!*"
And we all called out for more! -
When Frankie Vaughan kicked his way through that "*Green door –o!*"

The 'Six five special' and 'Oh boy' to us kids were as cosmic
As the 'whiz bang' you got free with the 'Beezer' comic
"*Got the one and only walkin' talkin' living doll*'
Sang Cliff & the Shads – "Rrrubbish!" grumbled our 'square' dads
As they turned on the 'Dave king show'
We screamed – "*Don't you rock me dad-dy-*o"

"*She's my Tallahassee lassie*" raged Freddie Cannon
As Don Lang and his Frantic Five sang
'My Friend the Witch Doctor went -
"*Oo-ee-oo-a-a-ting-tang-walla-walla-bing-bang*'"

When the girls swooned over *'Dream lover'* Bobby Darin
& sang Connie Francis songs like – *'Lipstick on Your Collar'* -
'Stupid Cupid' & *'Carolina Moon'*
& little miss dynamite - Brenda Lee's *'Sweet Nothin's'* -
mostly out of tune!

Us lad's sang Eddie Cochran tunes
Like *'Come on Everybody'* & *'Summertime Blues'*
"*Giddy-up-a-ding-dong*" by Freddy bell & the Bell boys
& Larry Williams's - "*I've gotta girl called Bony Maronie*
She's gotta figure like a stick of macaroni"

That sent 'shivers down the backbone'
And made our parents quake & quiver with fright
As us spotty teenagers 'shake, rattled & rolled away the night
The older Teddy boys Jailhouse rocked around the clock'
In their blue suede shoes - with 'pretty, pretty, pretty Peggy Sue's'

We bopped to -
"*Beee-bop-a-lula-she's my baby*
Be-bop-a-lula- I don't mean maybe"
By Gene Vincent & the Blue Caps

We jived to Little Richards's-
Rutti tutti & Long tall sally
We were 'teenagers in creation'
As we sang these rock n roll songs
Down our alley

These were *'Magic moments'*
'The story of my life'
'On the street where I lived'
'Memories were made of this'

While Lonnie Donegan
Was *Putting on the Style*
& Johnny Duncan
& his Bluegrass Boys
Were taking the
Last train to san Fernando

& Elvis was staying at the
Heartbreak Hotel
- We were takin' an ol' trolley
To go 'coal pickin' on Clayton tip

22

1959

Feb 3rd. 1959
Was another sad year for us little Rock & Rollers'
'Buddy Holly' was killed along with the 'Big Bopper'
& 'Richie Valance' in another tragic air disaster

Eddie Cochran should have been on the same tour but for some reason didn't go -
Ironically he was killed a year later in a car crash while touring Britain in April 1960
With Gene Vincent who survived with bad head & leg injuries
It was such a great loss

We were devastated by the bad news - all our heroes, first our football team
Manchester United then our Rock & Roll idols seemed fated to die so young -
How would we cope?
I had a permanent lump in my throat in those early pre-teen years

RADIO

'Educating Archie' (Andrews)
With Peter Brough
The 'Radio' ventriloquist act? -
You couldn't hear his lips move! -
What a twist!
Then when T.V. came out -
They vanished in the mist

On the wireless (radio)
We had the weird & wonderful surreal
Goon Show what a team-
Spike Milligan, Peter Sellars,
Harry Seacombe & Michael Bentine

'Hancock's Half Hour'
& 'The Clithero Kid' brought tears to our eyes
'The Archers' & 'Mrs Dale's Diary' for the old & wise

'Two way Family Favourites'
With requests from the forces abroad
'Dick Barton' - special agent
The space adventures of 'Dan Dare'
'The Man in Black' with Valentine Dial -
Would raise your hair

Wakey waaaaaakey! every Sunday afternoon
Bellowed 'Billy Cotton' & his Band
You had 'Edmundo Ross' & his Latin American sound
"Lacuccaracha-Lacuccaracha
Cackycackycackybum"– this made our Gran swoon.

And if you tuned into (with great difficulty) to the crackly
'Radio Luxembourg' - our favourite rock & roll station
You would hear the voice of 'Horace Batchelor'
Of Keynsham - spelt: k - e - y - n - s - h - a - m
Selling his so called 'Pools' formula and plan
He used to take a cool 10% of any winnings you got - what a con!
Not bad odds when you're bound to get the odd win in a million

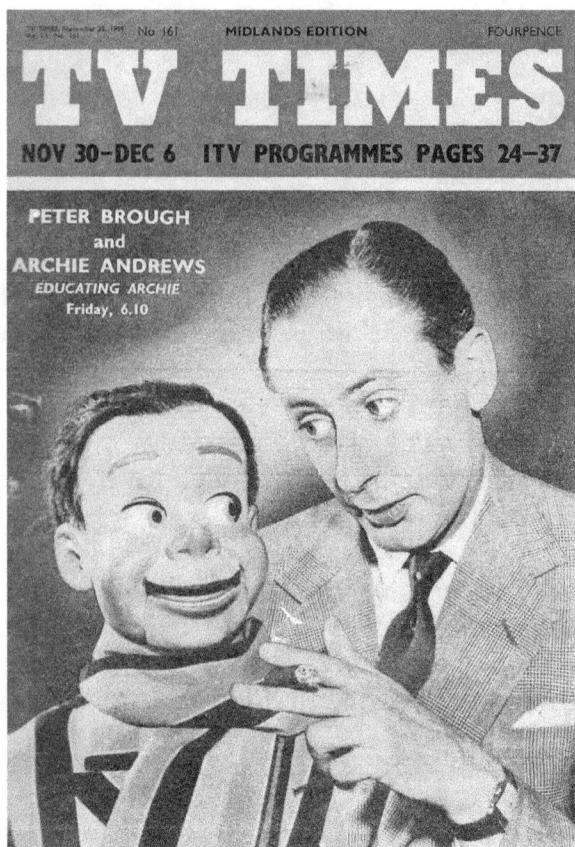

THE FLICKS

Friday nights - going to the Flicks
The 'Carlton' in Clayton – the 'New Royal' in Bradford
The 'Mosely' (moko) & the 'Don' in Beswick were the local 'Flicks'

Matinees at the 'Carlton' on a Saturday afternoon
For a 'tanner' each you were rewarded with
Flash Gordon's trip to mars with Buster Crabbe
Three Stooges - Abbot & Costello - Marx Bro's - Laurel & Hardy
Hopalong Cassidy - 'clipperty clipperty clop' ...

Tarzan the ape-man - King Kong, Lassie & Rin Tin Tin - hero hounds
The mark of Zorro - Looney Tunes plus a feast of Wait Disney cartoons.

Those singing cowboys (and cowgirls) -
Tex Ritter (on his horse white flash)
"Home, home on the range" - Sang Gene Autry
(On Champion - the wonder horse)
And Roy Rodgers (on trigger) singing "A four legged friend -
A four legged friend, he'll never let you down"

Annie Oakley and Calamity Jane starred
The blond bombshell - Doris day
Singing the 'Deadwood Stage' song -
"Oh! whip crack away, whip crack away, whip crack away"

Buffalo Bill - Wild Bill Hickock - Wyatt Earp - Billy the Kid - Davy Crockett -
King of the wild frontier - Jim Bowie with his famous knife - Daniel Boone -
Pioneers of the American civil war films - the Buccaneer and
The Red Badge of Courage with - Audie Murphy who had more medals
On his chest than 'my brother Silvest'.

And apart from those corny 'carry on' films
& latest craze '3D movies'
We saw great war films like - Camp on Blood Island
The Dambusters - The Cockleshell Heroes - The Longest Day
The Wooden Horse - Bridge on the River Kwai - The Red Beret

John Wayne (as Davy Crockett) - in The Alamo was super
So was Alan Ladd in 'Shane'
Remember 'High Noon' with Gary Cooper - "Do not forsake me -
Oh! my darling sang Tex Ritter in high refrain

That great musical - 'Singing in the Rain'
With Gene Kelly - Donald O'Connor - Cyd Charisse
Debbie Reynolds had us all dancing insane

Those Biblical epics - Exodus - The Robe
The Ten Commandments - The Greatest Story Ever Told
With Charlton Heston - Burt Lancaster - Richard Burton - Jean Simmons
Ben Hur - Spartacus - The Vikings and Hercules
With muscle-men Victor Mature, Kirk Douglas and Steve Reeves

Gina Lollobrigida - Audrey Hepburn - Brigitte Bardot
Ava Gardner - Sophia Loren - Elizabeth Taylor - Marilyn Monroe
Enhanced our fantasies to the extreme
As we compared ourselves with that giant
And 'rebel without a cause' hero - James Dean.

Then as we got a bit older - fourteen or so
We used to go to a certain Cinema - the 'Queens' (in Ardwick)
That was renown to us under-aged spotty teenagers
To let you in for X's –

Those hot horny sex films like 'Naked as Nature Intended'
(which was actually a Naturist film) & World by Night
Gave you the most erotic dreams at night!

Then those hairy scarey horror films -
I, Was a Teenage Werewolf - The Incredible Shrinking Man
The Gorgon - Godzilla - The Blob and 'It' - From Outer Space'
That made your hair turn white with fright!

I remember my first X - Quatermas's Experiment -
I ran all the way home with a lump in the back of my trousers

THE WILD 'NORTH WEST'

Cowboys and Indians were the vogue of the fifties T.V.
Programmes were inundated with them -
The Cisco Kid with Pancho Villa
The Lone Ranger and Tonto - *keemosabbii!*

Wells Fargo - Sugarfoot - The Man From Laramie
Range Rider with 'all american boy' - Dick West
Gunsmoke - Lawman - Colt 45 - Branded - Have Gun, Will Travel
- Rawhide and Wagon Train were the best

Cheyenne Bodie - Bronco Lane – Bonanza
& of course Champion the Wonder Horse
Lassie and Rin Tin Tin
Maverick - with Bo, Bart and Brett
Have all disappeared into the sunset

With a battered old 'Trilby' as a cowy hat
A hanky tied around your neck and pulled up to your nose
A 'Lonestar gun and holster' with silver spurs
A Lassoo made up of mum's old washing line -
As you lassooed the dog or the occasional feline

Pulling and tugging on our imaginary reins and
Slapping the sides of our bums incessantly
As we galloped down the streets of our locality

- With a speed of light and a
Cloud of grime & dust
We rode into the wild,
Wet & windy Northwest -
"Hi! –Ho! - Silver! Awaaaaaay!"
Cries the cowboys of yesterday

MONDAY - WASHING DAY

Battling & tussling
With the old kitchen Boiler, Mangle & Dolly Tub
With Omo - Rinso - Oxydol & Miracle Acdo washing powders
Was our mum on the Washboard creating the rhythmic sound —

A Rub! Rub! Rub! A Rub! - a Scrub! Scrub! Scrub!
Ringing & rinsing. squeezing & squelching - what a chore!
Turning the 'stiff-as-buggery' handle on the Mangle
With soap suds splashing & spilling onto the kitchen floor.

And us kids slipping & sliding
Allover the place

"Bryan! - Duncan! - Glyn!   -
Philip! - David!
- You'll get a 'thick ear'

& I'll slap yer legs 'red raw'
If you don't behave!'

No wonder mum threw
A wobbler & had a fit -

She must have had muscles
In her spit!

With the clothes drying out on the 'Rack'
Water dripping & trickling down your back
& all the 'ironing' yet to abuse
No wonder mum had the 'Dolly Blues'

GOIN' ERRANDS

THE CHIPPY –

Dad's treat every Friday week
Was to embrace us with 'six-a-chips' with fish --
Battered cod, haddock or silver hake
Fried in beef dripping
With a great dollop of mushy peas
It was the bee's knees

I being the eldest, had to go for our weekly treat
And as the years went on and on
And my family kept expanding on
My list became longer and longer
From three, four, five, six and finally seven fish
Depriving the fishing population for our Friday dish

All wrapped up 'nice an' snugly" in newspaper
Hopefully the sports pages
Of the football pink or green
With a picture of our famous football team!
Gettin' a bag of 'scratchings' for free
Was a just reward for little ol' me.

Also goin' to the Butcher's every Saturday mornin'
For three Lamb chops an' half a pound of beef dripping
Then four, five, six & eventually seven chops an' a pound of dripping
Was another errand of mine
And I didn't get any extra spends for overtime

A VISIT TO MY GRANDMA'S

As grandad empties the ash can and fetches the coal bucket in
To my fascination - I'd watch grandma, wistfully making
'Curlers' by the Hearth - the practising art of 'origami'.
Placing them inbetween the coal, coke and firewood
Followed repetitiously by sweeping the grate, lighting the curlers
Pushing the damper in - pulling the damper out
Putting the blower up -

Or placing a sheet of newspaper spread-eagled
And held up by the shovel - what a ritual!
Sometimes catching fire & spreading instant panic
To the household .

When all was settled, we'd sit by the fireside
Grandma in the best armchair darning grandad's ol' socks
Grandad at the writing bureau studying his football coupon
Or reading his bible - the football green
And me on a big cushion

Then grandma would tell me wondrous stories
About her Childhood days - the olden days -
The depression was her favourite then came the wars -
First the second - then the first

About how grandad got wounded in the arm
In the bloody battle of the 'Somme'
And how they all huddled up together under the table
Petrified in pitch darkness during the air raids

Sitting there, mouth agape, listening intently, staring fixedly
Into the blazing hot fire's glowing embers -
Watching the red, yellow & blue flames
Flickering – spiraling – entwining – dancing
I was spellbound – engrossed - entranced - locked in the past!

"Come along now young un' -
You must be gerrin' off 'afore it get's dark" she'd always say
Slipping my 'Balaclavar' over my head and fastening my coat.

Then grandma would stand outside her front door
To wave me off -
Down our street until I got home

At night, alone in my bed
I often dreamt and wished
That I'd have lived in those bygone days
Those exciting olden days
Those wondrous days of yore

GRANDAD & GRANDMA

ALL THE DAY TO DREAM

Look at him sitting there
On the edgings without a care
Ragged-arsed little kid
His grubby little finger curling his hair

Daydreaming and imagining
He was on a distant planet somewhere
Like Flash Gordon, Buck Rodgers & Dan Dare

Floating through a time tunnel he'll go
Disappearing & reappearing in a Tardis like Dr. Who
Marooned on a desert island like Robinson Crusoe.

Look at him, sitting there
Ragged-arsed little kid
Staring at his reflection in an old tin lid
Wondering, fantasising, visualising

He'd dream-
Playing for his favourite football team
Lead singer in a rock & roll band
A big star of the movie screen

Look at him, sitting there
Snotty-nosed, tatty hair
Having the time of his life
Unconsciously digging up moss
Inbetween the flagstones
With a rusty old pen knife

Look at him, sitting there
Dropping handfuls of stones down a dirty old grid
Daydreaming and imagining
He could fly like superman,
Climb a building like Spiderman
To be lord of the jungle like Tarzan
Wishing he was lost in a sweet factory and never found

Experiencing the thrill of falling
Thro' a hole in the ground like
Alice in Wonderland

Flying on a magic carpet around & around
A Peter Pan in Never Never land
Or a cartoon character in Disneyland

Look at him, sitting there, little boy lost
But without a care
Lost in imagination, lost in a dream, lost in a stare

MY LITTLE BROTHER 'BUGGERLUGS'

Like a clapped out 'Wells Fargo' stagecoach trots
Granelli's 'orse an' cart up our street
Tooting an' honking his horn
To the clatter an' patter of tiny feet

Wafers, lollies, ninety nines and twists
'Any broken wafers' pleads a little urchin in distress
"Ere you are son' he'd reply, pretending to shake his fist
- Now bugger off, smartish!'

Then off he'd retreat
Leaving his trademark -
'Shredded wheat' like 'orse droppings
Stinkin' & steamin' in the street

Mams & dads armed with shovels, buckets & sacks
Would swoop (like vultures preying on carrion)
& scoop it all up - to fertilise their little front gardens
& window boxes outside their back to backs'

"Listen young un' dad would joke
If you put a shovel full in each shoe
You'll grow to six foot two!"

Anyway, this particular hot sunny, summers day
A freshly laid batch of
'Shredded wheat' like 'orse droppings as usual lay
Stinkin' & steamin' in the street

& before our mams & dads could gather pace
Out shoots my little brother (Dunc) with his cricket bat
And in a mad frenzy
Whacks, smacks & bats them all over the place

Well, my cousin's boyfriend
(who usually wasn't very car cleaning conscious)
Had just cleaned his car inside and out
& had left his boot open – "Oh! No!" - he'd shout

"Hell fire! - I don't bloody believe it! Oh!! Shit!!!"
With other choice expletives spewing from his lips
His boot was being filled rapidly by my little brother
Who was now concentrating all his efforts into it

"Ssstopp!! Yer little bugger - I'll bloody kill yer!"
He was yellin' and bawlin' an' goin' all purple with rage
"If I get mi 'ands on yer - I'll *#*@*#*! you!- he'd go on,
Jumping over the gate - getting ready to chase
The little 'scallywag' of six years of age

But my little brother who was goin' all pale & weak
Had other ideas -
With one terrifying look,
Drops his bat
& wi' little legs going
Like the clappers -
Tear-arses off
Down our street

MISCHIEF

Playing 'black & white rabbit'
(knocking on doors & running away)
Or tying two door knockers together -
Pulling the string, hiding, watching, sniggering
At them struggling to open their front doors
- Until the string snapped of course

Phone tapping (press button a - press button b)
Was also rife - sifting through the Telephone Directory
Looking up funny names
And saying unfunny things
Like 'gerroff the line there's a train coming'

I remember going to the Pantomime
At the Manchester Hippodrome
To watch Norman Wisdom
We were high up in the stalls
Throwing 'sherbet lemons' & mint balls
At the poor ol' orchestra for a lark
We just laughed and laughed
Watching them ducking & diving for cover
Looking really silly & daft

Playing 'wag'
With my mate
Little Wragg
Until we were found out
By the School Board -
Extra homework &
Lines were the reward

Some kids used to play
'Chicken on the line'
Until one poor boy
Was Killed -
He was only nine

MY LITTLE BRO'S DUNCAN & BRYAN

36

FIGHT?

"My dad can fight your dad!"

"Oh! no! he can't!"

"Yes he can! - he used to box for the Army - you know!'

"Oh! yeh! -
Well my dad used to wrestle alligators in the jungle!

"Oh, yeh!"

'"Yeh!

Well! my mum will box your dad's ears off!'
"Right - I'm gonna tell!!' - "Murmurmamurma!'

SCARLET FEVER

Asian flu, Polio, Dyptheria & Whooping cough
Were the 'in diseases' in the Fifties
We had to be vaccinated (or have the prick) to combat them
We also had regular visits from 'Nitty Nora' the jungle explorer
Whenever there was an outbreak off Nits in the school

I remember being stricken with scarlet fever
Being laid up, feeling quite sick & sorry for myself
Not being able to play out for weeks on end ...

Neighbours & friends sent me comics & annuals to read
Being spoilt rotten & waited on hand and foot
By my Mum & Dad, wasn't too bad

Being off school & missing my *'eleven plus' exam*
I suppose deprived me of a better chance - what a sham!
Having to take it at a different school
Without any proper preparation & instruction
Was an unfair, unintelligent situation
Branding kids like me a failure by
A system created by fools

Thank god it's no longer recognized
It's no way to assess your intelligence & cleverness
By diversifying between failure & success
On an eleven year old's shoulders
- Of whose the best on one pathetic memory test

DAD'S FIRST CAR

Dad's first car was a 1936 Austin ruby saloon
And cost dad £100.00 - we were over the moon
A real car - we were posh
The affluent family - oh! golly gosh!

Our pals will think we're snobs - what!
Will it affect our street cred - I think not. ..

It was a spiffing, jolly super, little car
Although it wouldn't take us very far
With real leather seats to sit on
And a photo of 'Lonnie Donegan' stuck on the back window
We were off - bbbbbbbrum! wheels in motion - to – oblivion!

WAITING FOR DAD COMIN' HOME FROM WORK

Down on one knee
His strong arms outstretched
As I ran down our street to greet him
Smelling strongly of engine oil and elbow grease
His neatly folded newspaper in his overall pocket
His beaming smile, his thick auburn curly hair
Ruddy complexion and shiny forehead
"What-ave-ya-got-me-from-work dad?"
As he pulls out a newly machined 'magnet' from his butty bag
"'Aww!! bazzin!! - fanks dad!
Just what i've always wanted!"
As he carried me off shoulder high
All the way home with a mischievous glint in his eye

SUNDAY SCHOOL

Our parents used to encourage (elbow) us kids
To go to the Methodist Mission every Sunday
Dressed in our black blazers
And 16 inch bottom grey flannel trousers - yes grey!

I used to hate those 16 inch grey flannels with seams
Especially when the style was skin-tight jeans
I remember cutting them up one day
To our parents shock and dismay
It was worthwhile being grounded for a week or so
You see - those flannels had to go man go

At Sunday school we would sing peaceful & passive hymns
Like 'Fight the good fight with all thy might'
'Onward Christian soldiers marching as to war
With the cross of Jesus going on before'
And 'Heee would true valiant be 'gainst all disaster
L a - l a - la - la - la - la aaa - let him constant be, follow the master'

Being one of God's little sunbeams & Devil hater
I would naturally think of heaven & the 'hereafter'
Although sometimes I would be a little bored
Yyyyawn! and think of 'out there' later

Every Sunday 'religiously' we were sent
And we had to have our 'star cards' stamped to prove that we went
Putting potential 'sweet money' into the collection box
& thinking of 'Nuttal's Mintoes' brought a lump to my throat
As we finished off with the Lord's prayer
I used to sigh and thank God for letting us out of there

BOY SCOUTS

Joining the 'Johnson & Yewlette' local Boy Scout Troop
As both 'cub' & 'scout' and being affiliated to 'stag' group was
A phase that most kids went through
A sense of adventure, a uniform with badges, a scout knife
And lots of weird and wonderful things to do -

Playing 'British Bulldog' was hard and tough
Scouting, camping & hiking sometimes got tiring and rough
Collecting waste paper and empty bottles for charity
Getting involved with the 'gang show' variety

Doing the cub and scouts salute - three fingers then two
Chanting the 'Scouts Honour'
"Akala - we'll do our best for God and the Queen"
Such patriotism, all loyalist and squeaky clean

Getting tied up in all kinds of knots -
The clove hitch, half hitch, sheepshank and reef knots
Passing your 'Tenderpad' then 'Tenderfoot'
Going on to be a third, second and first class scout
We'll Dyb! Dyb! Dyb! and we'll Dob! Dob! Dob!'
Then we'd go touting for 'bob a job'
Wondering what a 'ging-gang- gooly-gooly-gooly-gooly
Watcha-ging-gang-goo-ging-gang-goo' - was or meant?

As we sang and had 'jamborees' by the campfires outside the tent.
Going on parade and marching with the 'Scholars'
Snarling at the 'Boys Brigade', pulling faces at the 'Brownies'
And lech'in' & leerin' after the 'Girl Guides'

My mates used to whistle and clap, taunt & tease me -
'Cos I had to wear khaki shorts - 'til I could take no more abuse –
So! - It was off with the neckerchief, woggle & beret & on with -
The ice-blue skin tight jeans, mohair sweater & winkle-picker shoes
And girls, girls, girls!!!

WHIT WALKS

Us kids called scholars walked in processions
Down the main roads of our localities
Vivacious young girls - a little embarrassed
Wave nervously at highly polished and proud parents

Brass Bands blarting - Pipers piercing
Scouts thumping – Boys Brigades blaring
Crowds pushing - Girl Guides blushing
All looking exceedingly proud
All playing excitingly loud

Crucifix's high - Banners sway and ripple in the wind
Proddy's and Catholics - Methodists missions
The Sally Army and old soldiers
March with dignity on this weekend

Mums & Dads - Uncles & Aunts
Brothers & Sisters - Sons & Daughters
Waving of hands - clapping emphatically
All filled with exhilaration & jubilation on this day

All in their best attire - right down to their socks
Italian style suits - flamboyant hats - best flowery frocks
Winkle-pickers - chisel toes shoes - stiletto heels were in fashion
Everybody looked absolutely smashin'

Grown ups popping the odd 'two bob piece' or a 'shilling'
(the tight ones - a 'tanner')
Into your suit top pockets - you made a killing!

With ice cream all down your tie
Sticky toffees in your pocket
As you carried that back-breaking banner
That swayed and always seemed to be against the wind
Sometimes you nearly took off - like a rocket!

Even worse - if you were ladened with the lamb
Which you carried 'til yer arms were droppin' off

43

Those tailenders -
Stiff-necked red faced drunks and deadlegs
Staggering and marching out of step and tune
To the crowds amusement - they were over the moon ...

All the pubs were heaving
And so were our dads - later in the evening
Everybody was happy having a great night
Just the occasional Proddy & Catholic fight

It brought the neighbourhood together
The odd bitching over each others new clothes
A little bit of jealously - I suppose.

This was the tradition - our tradition
Carried on through generations
It was like 'Cup Final' day -
A great day out for all the family
Yet sadly, nowadays it seems to have lost its way

SCHOLARS

THE KERRY PIPERS

AND THE DREADED LAMB

TOGGER

I remember when we used to play sides down our street
Using pullovers & coats as goalposts
Or between the lamp-post & the end terraced wall

Sometimes the ball would rocket off the lamp-post
Through somebody's front window - smash!
We'd all leg it over the croft in a flash.

"You'll-pay-for-yer-own-china!"
Pleaded one frightened minor
In case we were caught and had to pay
Especially as the culprit was by now approximately 10 miles away

Playing football in those old brown boots with a leather 'casey' (case ball) -
When it got wet it was as heavy as lead
Sometimes when you jumped to head the ball
You ended up semi-conscious with an impression
Of the laces embedded in your forehead

Thank god for the 'Frido' (plastic ball)
Which was much softer and safer to head - well!
Although sometimes when it smacked against the back of your legs
Or hit the side of your face it stung like hell.

I remember those stylish 'Real Madrid' football boots
Coming into fashion - Di Stefano - Puskas - and me! -
I bought a pair from ex-Man United famous footballer
Johnny Aston's sports shop which was in our locality

Next to the famous 'Gramophone Lounge' toy shop
Where us kids would ogle the window as we claimed our toys in turn -
"Bags that! Bags this! Bags that! Bags this! Bags that!" -
We'd barter 'til as our vivid imaginations ran away with us

OUR CUP FINAL

Top of the street - Clarkes & Platty's lot versus
The bottom - Wood's & Wraggy's lot
On the infamous 'red rec' football pitch ...

On our side we had - Ged 'the 'Ed ' Platt
Who used to head medicine balls for practice
Even threw bricks up in the air to let them
Split in half over his hard head

His brother Jacky who was a little more refined
And a stylish 'Albert Quixall' look-a-like player
Both played for the East Manchester area team

We had 'shirt tugger' Tommy Clarke - you didn't argue with him
He'd gIve you a terrific left uppercut if you did
Which left you reeling for days

His brother Franky the 'Teddy Boy'
And younger brother Joey who had no sense of danger at all
No nerves - nothing!
I think they ripped whatever nerves he had - out at birth!

'Piggy Smith' who hit the ball about 500 yards in front of him
And would leg after it about a million miles an hour to catch it
He was on the wing of course
He always seemed to lose the ball for us all

The dazzling dribbling hall brothers - Geoff and Bill,
Nobby 'Rocket Shot' Hughes, myself and my 'all left foot' brother Phil
In goals we had Jeff Platt - brother of 'Adge' the 'hacker'
Jeff was built like a brick-chicken house
He actually played for Man City juniors.

The opposition was quite awesome too
Especially the Wraggs - a couple of which played
Semi and professional football
The Woods with Tom and Wilf - who used to dribble
And disappear up his own bum

47

The games were played with such intensity
Like the Derby match between United & City

These fast and furious games
Went on and on for at least three hours or more

Until you couldn't see the ball any more
With the score about fifteen all
& with some of the goals being disputers
Arguing & squabbling all the way home
'Cos nobody wanted to be losers

For match practice we'd play 'three pots in'
Using Doctor Taylor's big bright orange garage door as the goals
Or heading practice from one side of the pavement to the other
Keeping the ball off the ground for hours and hours

And 'wallee' - hitting the ball as hard as you could
Against an end terraced wall
Causing havoc and pandemonium to the house owners
As they told us to scarper off sharpish
To us unselfish kids - they were just being old groaners!

GANG WARFARE

Gang rivalry was rife in the Fifties
You had to be hard and look really mean
My mate Eddie C - was a dead ringer for James Dean!
He had no 'bone' in his nose - his advantage being
When somebody 'stuck one' on him - he never flinched
Shook his head then gave his dumbstruck opponent a good kneeing

Although I had my hair greased up with Brylcreme
And had a quiff and d.a.
(some kids used butter for grease and some used lard)
Had my collar up and wore skin-tight jeans
With my winckle-pickers on - I walked bow-legged
And squinted my eyes - I still didn't look mean or hard
Cos' I had a baby face to my mate's disgrace

Nutting was the hallmark of violence -
I remember sticking the nut on one gang rival
And telling him - to get round the corner fast
Or else I'd really give him what for!

Then watching him skip and tootle off quite nonchalantly
As I grimaced and held my head in my hands - 'Ooh! the pain'
As I went home half conscious with a bad migraine

The big battle was the annual one against the Newt' neather's
Over the 'Lime Hills' on 'Clayton Dingle'
I've witnessed absolute loons running up those hills
wielding axes & hammers amidst hails of stones and shingle

SCHOOL DAYS

Those little oak desks with pot inkwells attached
A wooden pen with a nib that sabotaged your writing
Making it grow all furry and blotchy

Thus spoiling your masterpiece as you used your
Pink blotting paper to soak up that black inky mess
Although you could make great ink pellets
For flicking (with your ruler) at each other with
Nudging & smudging was quite common in Class

Chanting of the 'times tables' was a daily occurrence
& in certain classes the bible - Genesis - Exodus, etc

CANTEEN FOOD

Ice-cream type scoops of mashed & liquidised 'spuds'
Lumpy custard with roly-poly pudding
Manchester tart & spotted-dick
Prunes with semolina & tapioca -
Anything awful to make you sick

Thank God I went home for my dinner
Although after eating barley stew with a dumpling
Followed by home-made apple pie & rice pudding
Then legging it back to school for football practice

In which I always got a stitch & doubled up in pain
Quite often the lads would shout -
"What's up Press! - rice pudding?"
As I lifted up my head grimaced & nodded – "afraid so - aaaarrgain!"

CORPORAL PUNISHMENT

Mr.P, - couldn't sound his 'r' s
"Cywil get me that swipper" - he would command
Cyril being the classroom swot & teacher's pet
Of course was always at hand

Mr R. - a 'Jimmy Edwards' look-a-like - who was
Hailed as the master of the black leather strap
With three throbbin' tails
He used to bet you thre'pence that you couldn't
Move your outstretched hand away
Before he strapped it - oooouch! - he never failed

Then there was **Mr G**. he was so big & powerful
When he gave you the size 12 slipper
He called 'Oscar' - you would shoot across
The whole length of the class
With an extremely stinging sore arse

And then there was **Miss W**.
Who couldn't master the strap & her co-ordination
She often missed your hand
And hit her own leg with frustration
The kids used to laugh & snigger
As her face turned redder and redder

MR. R

There was the occasional winger across the back of your thick-head

When you played
The class fool
Or your knuckles rapped
Viciously with a
Wooden rule

THE SCHOOL HALL

ASSEMBLY

 "All 'fings bright and beautiful all creatures great and small'"
& "we plough the fields and scatter the good seed on the ground"
We sang in our monotone Manc accents - what a horrible sound!!
"All good (girls) around us are sent from heaven above -
Oh 'fank the lord oh 'fank the lord for all all allll his love"

GAMES IN THE HALL

We used to play crab football and matt rugby
Where the soft kids got kicked from pillar to post
& where you were given the opportunity to charge and hack
The lads you disliked the most

BOXING PRACTICE

Was another excuse you had for duffin' that toe-rag you hate
Although when you had the opportunity to box his ears off
You kind of respected him and ended up being his best mate

We had the best boxing team in the Manchester area
In the late fifties and early sixties
Our school team Ravensbury street won the -
'Manchester Evening News' Boxing trophy on many occasion ...

We had the blistering Bebbington bro's, the mighty Monk's bro's,
The artistic Allen bro's, the rugged Wragg bro's ,dazzling Johnson bro's
We had knockout Nobby Hughes, jinkin' Johnny Burns
Battlin' Billy Hall, sugar Ray Blencoe & duckin' n divin' Dave Blakeley
To represent our winning team

THE FAMOUS BOXING TEAM WITH TEACHER'S MR. 'TED' REARDON (left) & MR. ROBINSON (right)

Plus one kid who won a medal without ever having a bout 'Alf Gratton' -
(3rd from the left) - he was so big nobody could match his weight -
Hence he'd have a succession of walkovers every fight

SCHOOL SPORTS DAY

Every year we had a big sporting occasion
At 'Belle Vue's super sports arena
Where all the schools in Manchester
Would compete in various track and field events

Also at school - we had our very own 'Sports Week'
The Long Jump - Broad Jump - High jump
(where the Fosbury flop changed his name to the Prestbury flop!)

Hop, skip and jump (or hobble, trip, and bump)
The shot put & 'chucking' the Javelin -
(over some poor bugger's backyard!)
100 yards - 200 yards - 400 yards - 800 yard Sprints

The Hurdles, Relay & Cross country
Which well and truly separated the boys from the girls

The 'Sportsboy of the Year' Trophy most years -
Was contested by either 'Ged Platt' or 'Nobby Hughes'
Both were excellent athletes
It was a great pity one of them had to lose!

Five a side football competitions In the schoolyard
Between the 'houses' - Hawk * Falcon * Swift * Eagle
Was another annual event us kids relished in

CHILD PRODIGY

I'm a mathematical genius
And at English - I'm the best
In Literature - I'm the wittiest
Like Oscar Wilde, I'm the prettiest

My art is like 'Renoir's' -
That brilliant Impressionist
In History- I'm a Napoleon
In my braces and string vest

I sailed around the world
In my Geography exam
Naming capitals of every country
From Alaska to Taiwan

You can't touch me at Science
So inventive, explosive & unique
In Gymnastics - you've guessed
The fittest with my superb physique

You see I've passed all my exams
And i've never failed a test
Top marks in every subject
Grades of the very best

Yes, being a right little swot & clever bugger
All smart an' smug - just ask my mum!
Oh! by the way - my IQ is -
Wait for it, you're absolutely right –
The absolute maximum!

SCHOOLYARD

I reflect on my schooldays - in our old schoolyard
Those hot, sweltering, sunny summer's days
To me - days that were long and forever
The phases - the crazes - whatever the season be -

A game of alleys (marbles) - no dob-handers of course!
But plenty of bad losers - which was worse
Catapults - ouch!! - spud guns - cap guns & bombs - pea-shooters
Yo-Yo's - water pistols that gave you a good soaking

Kingy - ticky off the ground - hopping johnny
Donkey rides - 'til the poor donkey was choking
Pile ups & scragging - tormenting & bragging
Donkey scrubs - Chinese burns - grazed knees
Paper Planes - flying saucers with sycamore leaves

Five a side football & basket ball
Cricket - chalking the wickets on the schoolyard wall
Bowling a hundred miles an hour with a corky ball

Those autumn conker fights -
(did you soak your sixes & niners in vinegar?)
Boasting about how many bangers you've got

Giving the bumps to the classroom swot
Ducking the teachers pet -
Down the toilet 'til he was all smelly & wet

And at wintertime -
Queuing & queuing for those sensational slides
Snowball fights (who put stones in their snowballs?)

Peeeeeep! the yard duty teacher blows his whistle
Once! - freeze – twice! - you run like hell to your 'form lines'

SMOKER'S CORNER

In our Schoolyard,
In our playground
Both dinner times and playtimes

You always found –
A smoker's corner -
Where us schoolkids
Would hang around

Having a sly drag and looking big
With our nicotine yellow-stained
Fingers clutching a cig,

Woodbines, Park Drive
Benson & Hedges ,
Player's Weights,
Senior service
Capstan full strength

Smoking & choking, coughing & splurting
Puffing those dimps 'til our fingers were burning

"Can yah! swallow?" - they would say
As you gently puffed away
And if you could without feeling dizzy
Turning green and being sick

You were big time! - one of the boys
One of the gang - in the clique!

'Til one day a little smart-arse bragged & said
"Can yah! blow smoke rings?"-
Tilting back his head & sending
The most incredible smoke signals

The Headmaster's way - with us kids standing there mouths agape,
Gob-smacked - knowing that the little pratt had given us all away!
 Yes - in our Schoolyard, in our old playground
Where the O.A S.U.(Official Adolescence Smokers Union) was lost & found

COCK OF THE SCHOOL

Bloodstained knuckles, face bruised and battered
Hair dishevelled, clothes torn and tattered
Stands our hero, our new leader

Dusting his cap, won his scrap
Shouldered high and nobody's fool
And proudly proclaiming himself *'cock of the school'*

Strutting bowlegged around the schoolyard
Squinting his eyes to make him look hard

Like the mighty Emperor Napoleon
His army would follow him
And those who wouldn't he'd push aside
Especially those that were mard and cried

Off he swaggers, his head held high
Oh my! How the teachers would try
To convert our hero in vain

"Mee! a soppy milk monitor! -
A bleedin' puffy prefect

They must be - in bleedin' sane
He'd shout & growl
Then spit & scowl

Just think of my reputation
My proclamation!

Then one day our hero met his match
Pleads that he wasn't quite up to scratch
A tremendous scrap - a close contest

But our Hero came out - second best
Lost his title and now disclaimed
'Ex-cock of the school' - he's re-proclaimed

Nobody wants to know him, his friends have all gone
To follow their new leader - their new Napoleon
Oh! Life's so cruel for our yesterday's hero - now today's fool
As he kicks a tin can and walks away from the school

HALLE ORCHESTRA

Every once in a while us rag-arsed kids
Would be taken by our school music teacher Mr.Goodall
To experience the classical sound of the world famous
'Halle orchestra' at the Free Trade Hall

Conducted by the famous Sir John Barbirolli
Although us kids would have preferred Sir 'Buddy Holly'
We were fascinated by Sir John's writhing & wriggling
Ridiculous waving of his baton and violent shaking
Of his snow white hair
Makin' us kids giggle & snigger
To our 'red faced' 'music teacher's despair

Excited by Beethoven's fifth
And Tchaikovsky's 1812 overture
With those exciting explosions & fireworks
That sent us kids in raptures
And had us all whistling, stamping our feet
And calling for an encore

It was a cultural revolution, a touch of class
A shock to the system for us snotty nosed kids
Of the working class

Sat on the school bus and making such a fuss
On our way back to school
Arguing & squabbling whether it was sissy, square or cool
To like this kind of music as well as rock & roll.

SCHOOL LIBERATION SONG

We're free! We're free!
Out of the gates o' Libertee

No more writing
No more sums

& no more whackin' on our bums

SCHOOL HOLIDAYS

As a family like most families of this era
We went on our 'jollies' to local Lancashire resorts
Like the whimsical and brash Blackpool & Southport -
Where you could play beach games like 'spot the sea'
North Wales was another destination, especially Rhyl & Colwyn bay

And for a day's outing -
Cycling on my mate's tandem to 'Daisy nook',
We peddled (or whoever was at the front would)
Up 'Pop Brew's' steep hill

With a couple of jam butties and a bottle of water
In your saddle bag - you were dressed to kill!
And if you ran out of water you could knock on any doors
For a top up, locals were always obliging of course ...

Up Daisy Nook we often visited the 'Planes scrap yard'
Or 'Crime Lake' - with the 'mysterious village under the Lake
That fascinated us kids to the extreme

Then we'd call at that little 'wooden shack' Cafe
That sold sweets, tiger nuts and Walls ice-cream ...

Then it was off - crab apple & blackberry picking
We were wild and free - skimming stones across the lake
Creating ripples and ripples of fun
Then we'd cycle down 'Bunkers Hill'
- As fast as hell!

Not forgetting the Fair at Easter time
Where every kid made a bee-line
With a face-full of toffee apple, candy floss
A coconut, a prized goldfish in each hand

- Remnants of having a good time

BRO'S DUNC, PHIL, GLYN & MYSELF BLACKPOOL 1962

BRO'S PHIL, GLYN & DUNC

THAT LITTLE WOODEN 'SHACK' DAISY NOOK

TRAIN SPOTTING

Train spotting at Clayton Bridge railway station, Berry Brow
As you came home engulfed in coal dust and soot
& a jotting pad full with names & numbers
From those super Steam trains

EXPLORING

We often sneaked into the the local Factories for a thrill
I remember when we climbed into Andersons rubber mill
They always had stock-piles of rubber balls in millions
Of sacks scattered everywhere
In which we stuffed in our pockets & jumpers
And ran excitingly to our lair

On one occasion we crept into a Mortuary out of morbid curiousity
Joey Clarke who was a bit of a dare devil pulled out a dead body
Panicked out of sheer fright, gasped, screamed, then legged it -out of sight

SPORT

Going to the match every other Saturday
With my mate Nobby Hughes
Me one week to watch the reds (united)
& with him the following week to watch the blues (City)
(just to please him)

And Cricket at Old Trafford in the summer season
With fantastic fast bowler Brian Statham
And great batsmen like Geoff 'noddy' Puller & Jack Dyson ...

Also wrestling, speedway & stock car racing at Belle Vue
Remember unbeaten wrestler's - Count Bartelli & The Mask
Belle Vue Aces champion speedway rider the late great Peter Craven
Top motor cycle rider - Geoff Duke
Stirling Moss was the motor racing boss

Collecting stamps, football programmes
Wrestling and speedway mag's
Buying records with my paper money & spends
& the occasional packet of fags

Filling scrapbooks with favourite pics
Collecting and swapping stacks & stacks of comics
Autograph hunting especially your football heroes
Like Tommy Taylor & Duncan Edwards

Life seemed simple & more fulfilling
No such thing as inflation or price increases
And you seemed to get lots & lots for your 'shilling'

LEFT TO RIGHT AUNTIE ALWYN, MUM, GLYN, PHILIP, MYSELF, DUNCAN & BABY BRYAN

BELLE VUE

Belle Vue amusement park & zoo
Was a fun day out for all the family

If you felt bold and brave & had no nerve
You could have a suicidal ride
On the 'Bobs' Roller coaster
As it sped about a million miles an hour

Up & down, this way - that way, fast & furiously
It screeched & screamed towards Hyde Road -
Then suddenly stop, drop & swerve
What excitement - what a thriller
Was this great wooden mechanical monster 'Godzilla'

The penny arcades, side stalls & shows, the dodgems
The fun house, hall of mirrors, gggghost train - whooooo!
The Ferris wheel carousel & merry go round
Which sometimes made you sick

Candy floss, toffee apples & pop corn
You didn't know you were born

Then it's off to the zoo - to view.
The baboon's pink & manky bum
Poor ol" warthog - face like a battered clog!
Smelly elephant house & bear pit - what a hum!

Screeching macaws & parrots, roaring lions
Hungry hippo's & rampant rhino's
Shy orang-u-tans, growling gorillas & pretty flamingos
Dainty deers, graceful gazelles, zebras & giraffes
And those horrible howling dingo's ...
Teasing the tigers and mimicking the monkey's

Especially the chimpanzees - who always peed on you just for a tease!

THE CIRCUS

Apart from the Clowns to us kids
The Circus was a bit boring
The Lion Tamers - Tight rope walkers -Trapeze artists
Acrobats & Knife throwers
Fire-eaters - Escapologists & Sword swallowers

Sea lions balancing beach balls on their noses
Dogs jumping through rings of fire
Elephants trooping around the arena trunks to tails
The Ringmaster - the Band in the bandstand
Did their best to entertain us

But we only went to please our mums & dads
Who unbeknown to us kids - also found it boring!
& took us kids because they thought we liked it as such
In fact, nobody really liked the Circus much

CLAYTON PARK

The 'rat-bag' on the 'Sea-saw' was a certain game
Where half a dozen kids stood at one end
& you at the other - if you were insane!

As they tossed you up & down like a rag doll
Fast & furiously until you fell off
Or cried out, 'I submit' in vain

Daring each other to -
Hang upside down on the 'Witches hat' & 'Round-a-bout' -
'til the blood rushed to your 'ed

& who could jump the furthest from the 'Swings'
Swing the longest on the 'Tarzan ropes'
Slide backwards on the Slides

And the most daring one of all was that dreaded 'Jerker'
Where two of you stood up & swung to & fro -
Higher & higher –

Faster & faster
'Til one of you felt whizzy & dizzy
Then inevitably threw up!

Every so often they'd have a 'Punch & Judy' show near Clayton Hall
Then off we'd go -
Creeping down the moat & up over the wall

We were alone? Inside that eerie, creaky, haunted, musty old Hall
& you always got somebody that sneaked up on you
& just at that tense moment - screamed 'Gotchaa!' or 'Booh!'

Scaring us all half to death
As we scuttled back over the moat
Gasping, white faced - all out of breath.

FRANK 'THE COCKY'

Frank the park keeper
Or 'cocky'
As us kids called him
amongst other names
Was a right character
That used to chase & hit you
With his 'stick' if you gave
Him cheek

I remember him hitting
My mate Joey Clarke
& breaking his 'stick' in two!
& barring him for a week

Then if you got really naughty
& he couldn't cope
He would send for 'Snowy' -

The Park Superintendent
Who was a red-faced, white haired, ferocious looking bloke
When his presence was felt – us kids would pelt

CLAYTON HALL - MY BRO'S DUNC & GLYN

STREET SONGS

Dan, Dan the dirty ol" man
Washed his face in a frying pan
Combed his hair with a donkey's tail
Scratched his belly
With his big toe nail

Billy Jones the bag
O'bones
Sailing down the river
A big fish come
An' bit his bum
And made his
Belly shiver

Solomon Grundy
Born on Monday
Christened
on Tuesday
Married on
Wednesday
Took ill on
Thursday
Worse On
Friday
Died on
Saturday
Buried on
Sunday
And that was the end
Soloman Grundy

Once upon a time
When the bird mucked the line
And the monkey
Chewed tobacco
And the little piggy run
With his finger up his bum
To see what was the Matter

Lulu had a baby
His name was
Sonny Jim
She took him
To the toilet
To teach him
How to swim
He swam
To the bottom
He swam
To the top
Just goin' under
When she grabbed him by his
Cock'tail whiskey 3/6 a bottle

Country girls are fancy country
Girls are slick
Put your arms around them
And they'll grab you by the –
Dicky was a bulldog
Lying in the grass
Along came a bumble bee
And stung him on the -
Ars'k no questions tell no lies
You never see a Chinaman
Buttoning up his -
Flies are dangerous
Bugs are worse
And this is the end
Of this silly little verse ..

BRO. GLYN

Yellow matter custard
Dead dog's eye
All mixed together
In green snot pie
Put it on a butty
Nice an' thick
Then cover it over
With a cup of cold sick – (yuk!)

GUY FAWKES NIGHT

'Hey mista! 'hav ya gorra penny for the guy?'
We'd cry as the drunks passed by
Sometimes they were so drunk
They often slipped us the odd 'half crown' piece by mistake
Straight in the back pocket it went - piece of cake!

Logging was both hard work & fun
Nicking back-gates & fences especially if you could run
Sneaking & creeping at night we'd go
Raiding the rival gang's wood
Dragging, carrying & scavenging as much as we could

Old prams, beds, sideboards, railway sleepers & rocking chairs
Looking for old coins, pens & rings
& many other exciting, precious things

On bonfire night - early on
We'd chase & throw penny bangers, tupenny cannons
& those terrifying rip-raps & deafening little demons
At the passing young girls - just for fun
Making them scream with fright - what a sight!

On the croft across the way
We'd light our bonfire - our very own display
First the paper then the wood
Blazing & burning - looking ferociously good

Then it's on with the guy -
Stuffed with old rags & straw - up he goes
Giving us one last sorrowful look & pleads -
As we sadly & sadistically watch him roar ablaze

Around the blazing hot bonfire sat on old benches & forms
Scoffing treacle toffee, hot chestnuts, baked spuds & parkin
Were our mums & dads, aunts & uncles, grandma's & grandads
Laughing, joking, singing & larkin'

What a spectacle!
Rockets and roman candles
Pin wheels, thunder flashes, rainbow fountains
Snow storms, blizzards & catherine wheels

Whizzing and whirling, flashing and flaring
And where the not so daring
Little tots and big soft kids
Stand trembling, eyes tightly closed holding their
Sparklers like magic wands In their shaking little hands

And as the nights air gets colder and colder
Our bonfire eventually starts to fizzle & smoulder
Then back to our homes we'd sadly go
To gaze through our bedroom window

With little eyes half-closing
Falling fast asleep until morning
Awakening just as it was dawning

We'd all venture out in the morning rain
Trying desperately to re-kindle
The crackling, smouldering debris
Of last night's bonfire - in vain!

CHRISTMAS

The glitter of tinsel
The glow of a candle
The glint in a child's twinkled eye
The glisten of gold & silver
Bells & baubles

The rattle & wrapping of gift wrap
The dazzle of dec's
The flicker of fairy lights
The whiteness of snow whiteness
The chinking of drinking glasses

Christmas is here

CHRISTMAS CONCERT

The best time of the year for us kids
Was the School Christmas party,
Carol service & concert
In the morning carol service we sang –

"In the bleak mid winter
Frosty wind made moan
Earth stood hard as iron
Water like a stone"

Snow had fallen
Snow on snow, snow on snow
In the bleak mid winter Lo-o-ong ago"

Followed mischievously by
"We three kings from Orient are
'One in a lorry and one in a car ,
One on a bicycle suckin' an
Icicle' following yonder star",
etc.

Then came –
'Ding dong merrily on high'
'O' little town of Bethlehem'
'Once in Royal David's City
& always finished with 'Silent Night

The Nativity play and
Christmas concert
Where all the kids with musical & theatrical talent
Would do their bit for England –

We had one 'hairy' school kid suddenly ripping off his shirt
Mimicking Neil Sedaka's song 'I go Ape'

Another little rock & roll guitar playing young 'un
Twanging & strumming the Ventures hit 'Walk don't run'
With our trendy art teacher on the drums

Then our class coming on one at a time
To the accompaniment of the piano -
Played by our Headmaster Mr. Jones

Singing – "Of all the 'fings I liked to be - I liked to be a -
Mine was would you believe it - a Policeman!

It went – "Of all the things I like to be
I like to be a policeman -

Repeat

Then 'blowin' mi whistle & stopping all the traffic
Blowin' mi whistle stopping all the traffic'

And doing the actions to the song – well! - I felt a right pillock!
Some of the other kid's were even worse - what a giggle
Anyhow we all had a reet good time - it was 'awright

The Christmas party always got out of hand though
We always ended up with a jelly & trifle fight

DAD'S WORK'S XMAS CONCERT

The Clayton Aniline. Co. 'Christmas party'
& trip to Belle Vue circus was a fantastic day out for us kids
After the traditional Turkey & Christmas pudd dinner
& being entertained at the Circus

We then got a large brown carrier paper bag full of goodies
With things like a Comic Annual book, Toy German Luger pistol,
Dinky car, Mask, Kazoo, Penny whistle
Party hat – usually a little Copper's or Fireman's helmet
A balloon, 'Der Der' (that thing you blow) & an apple & an orange
Plus a little white envelope with a 'tanner piece' (sixpence) inside

The cut off age for going to the party was twelve
But there was quite a few little urchins that were fourteen or so
masquerading (including my good self & Phil my younger bro.)
Well! wouldn't you? – it was a reet good do

CAROL SINGING

Carol singing in our nasal monotone
Manc accents was probably as bad as listening to
Somebody running their finger nails down a blackboard
No wonder we either got paid so quickly
Or told, on no uncertain terms, to sod off!

'Silent night' was our favourite
But unfortunately, not everyone else's
'While shepherds washed their socks by night'
Often went unnoticed .
'The twelve days of Christmas'
We never got past the second day
To our dismay

'0 come all ye faithful'
Was another favourite of ours
Especially the rousing chorus
0 come let us adore him'

'Ding dong merrily on high'
When we came to the 'gloooooooria' bit
That's when the bucket of water came as a direct hit. ..

If we were lucky we'd always finished with
'We wish you a merry Christmas'
We wish you a merry Christmas
We wish you a merry Christmas
And a happy New year'

A CHILD'S CHRISTMAS FEELING

On Christmas Eve the children say
We can't wait another day

Boys wait for their new toys
What do the girls want? - a sack of boys!

Bedtime comes the children pray

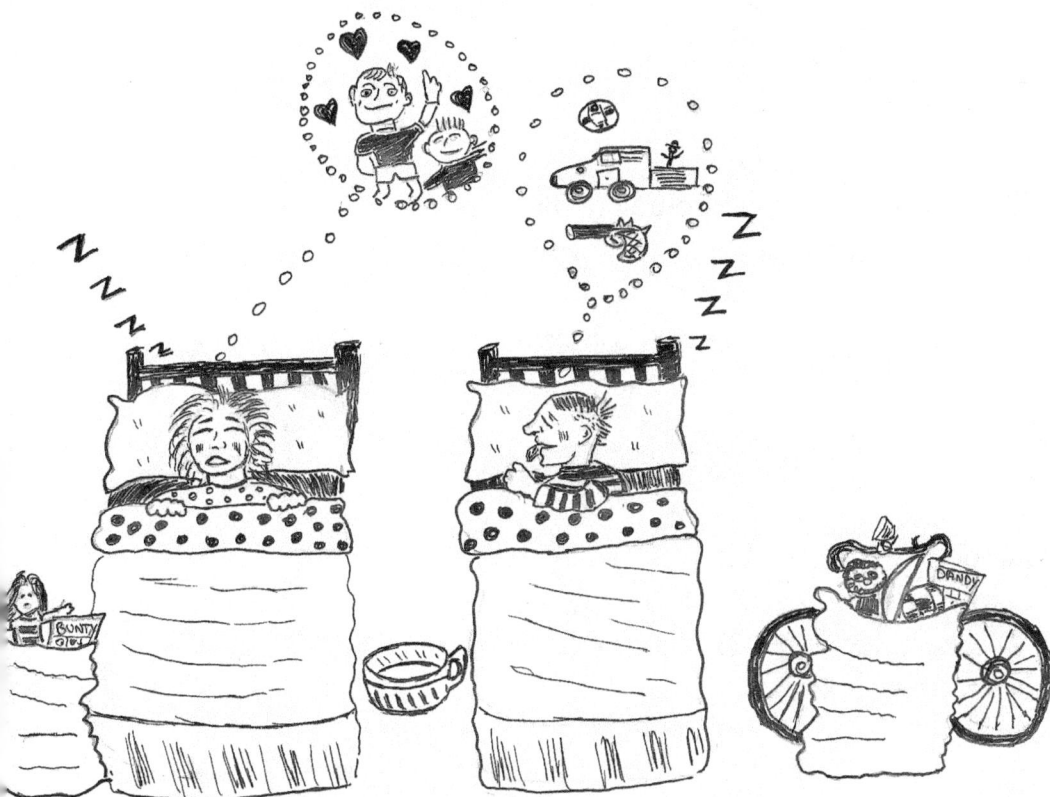

For baby Jesus was born this day

Tucked up in bed, fast asleep
Counting 'reindeers' instead of sheep!

Are they dreaming of their new toys?
Are the girls dreaming of their boys?'

Santa come - Santa go
On his sleigh through the snow

Children wake the morn. with cheer
'Cos they know that Christmas feeling's here

CHRISTMAS DAY

Our dad made forts, castles & garages -
A master craftsman was he!
& did up second hand bikes (for father Christmas)
To present to my brothers & me

Christmas morning was greeted with white pillow cases
Teeming with toys hanging over our bedsteads
Stockings draped - filled with apples, tangerines
Nuts & chocolate soldiers over the mantelpiece

Inside the pillow cases were -
Meccano sets - Bako sets - carpenter's tool sets
A pop gun - John Bull printing sets – Blow Football game
A Davy Crockett hat - a Jim Bowie knife? - maybe next year!

Cowboy outfit with silver spurs & a Lone star gun & holster
Lone Ranger mask - German luger - false moustache & beard
Indian outfit with feathered head-dress
A rubber tomahawk & dagger, moccasins plus a bow & arrow ...

There was Dinky - matchbox & Corgi cars
Lead soldiers - Kodak brownie camera - Dan Dare ray gun
Bus conductor's hat & ticket machine - Balsa wood gliders -
Fuzzy felt - activety books - Bagatelle
Mr. potato head & plasticine

Dandy - Beano & Rupert the Bear annuals - box of crayons
Monopoly - Ludo & Cludo board games
Selection boxes - Fry's tuck shop - a compendium of games
& if you were really lucky a Hornby double o train set
A Sunbeam Rapier bike or a Dansette

The rattling & ripping off of gift wrap was followed by
Ohhh! look at this, Ohhh! look at that – awe! look mum! hey dad!
Look what he's got me! – as Dad gave Mum a wink & a smile

The twinkle & glint of little eyes - was all worthwhile
The abundance of excitement - the magic of Christmas
& it always seemed to snow at Christmas in the fifties

A DANSETTE INTERCHANGEABLE RECORD PLAYER – WOW!

A COLD WINTER'S NIGHT

Snowflakes floating softly to the ground
Swirling & whirling around & around
A sensitiveness of quiescence overwhelms the night
Transcending it into a beautiful, moving, visual delight

What delicate symmetry each snowflake reveals
As it forms abstract patterns upon the garden trees
Contrasting with the pitch darkness of the night

The Streetlamps project shadows
That dance with delight

Depicting this drama, this scenario
Of a cold crisp & brisk winter's night

Freshly trudged footprints & car tracks that tease
The plight & flight of the virgin snow
As it falls caressing my bedroom window

Ponderous thoughts cross & open my mind
Wondering how sad for those who are blind

Yes - how sad not being able to see
This scene - this visual delight
That my eyes & yours can preciously see

DAVID PRESTBURY

Was born in Great Ancoats (Manchester 4) on the 8th June, 1948

Spent first two years of his life in Gorton, Manchester 18, England

Before family moved to Clayton, Manchester 11, in 1950 until 1963

Family then 'flitted' to Failsworth, near Oldham, Gtr. Manchester, England

Dave lived with his ex-wife, Carol, daughter Laura & son Jaimie

In 'posh' area of Whitefield near Bury, Gtr. Manchester

Has since moved back to Failsworth

He has two grown up sons, Damian & Nicholas from his previous Marriage

Also two grandchildren Robyn & Charlie

Attended Ravensbury Street Secondary school, Clayton, Manchester 11 until fifteen years of age

Joined printing industry as an apprentice compositor in 1963

To become a qualified Journeyman Compositor in 1969

Studied photographic printing techniques on 'Film Make up'

At College of Art & design Manchester 1969 –1970

Became disillusioned with his trade

Tried a variety of jobs: Postman, Production controller,

Progress chaser, Engineering Storekeeper/buyer

Dave has currently taken early retirement

& is now a full time Carer for his mother back in Failsworth

And has also become a full time writer -

His other interests include: Art – Drawing & Painting & Photography -

Previously had poems published in Various magazines

Allusions - Write On - Fly By Night, etc.

Been involved in a 'Road Show' (The Last Word) -

That evolved from The Commonword Writers' Workshop In Manchester

He has done readings at various Community Halls & Libraries

Folk Clubs & Night Clubs around the North West of England

Also Nottingham University & Belle Vue Peoples Festival in Manchester

Teamed up with fellow Poet & Road Show member & good friend
Alan Butterworth - they eventually joined **'The Valley Poets'**
To do 'Poetry & Pints' nights at the Organ Inn, Hollingworth, Hyde, Cheshire,
England in the early '80's Which involved doing a Variety Show called
'Pavement Artistes' at 'The Guide Bridge Theatre' in Ashton-under-Lyne,
Greater, Manchester, England

This is Dave's first collection (& special edition) of his autobiographical
Poetry which was first published in1998 by The Castle of Dreams
Publishing Co. Darlington, England

His second (follow up) book of autobiographical Poetry -
'Oasis & the Twisted Wheel' has been published through Lulu.com

And is set in the 'sexy' Sixties in & around the streets of Manchester,
England - Depicting the vibrant Club Scene & Street life,
Drawn from true life experiences & 'sex'sations'

He is currently writing a third book of Poetry —

Hidden by the Clouds – Deep Stuff

followed by a fourth book - **Sunny Side Up – funny stuff**

DAVID PRESTBURY 2008

www.ingramcontent.com/pod-product-compliance
Lightning Source LLC
La Vergne TN
LVHW081449070426
835509LV00014B/1507